Environmental Migrants

DAVE DALTON

Heinemann
LIBRARY

www.heinemann.co.uk/library
Visit our website to find out more information about Heinemann Library books.

To order:
 Phone 44 (0) 1865 888066
 Send a fax to 44 (0) 1865 314091
 Visit the Heinemann Bookshop at www.heinemann.co.uk/library to browse our catalogue and order online.

First published in Great Britain by Heinemann Library, Halley Court, Jordan Hill, Oxford OX2 8EJ, part of Harcourt Education.
Heinemann is a registered trademark of Harcourt Education Ltd.

Editorial: Jilly Attwood and Kathy Peltan
Design: Ron Kamen and Celia Jones
Illustrations: Jeff Edwards
Picture Research: Ruth Blair and Kay Altwegg
Production: Séverine Ribierre

Originated by Modern Age
Printed and bound in China by South China Printing Company

The paper used to print this book comes from sustainable resources.
10 digit ISBN 0 431 01383 7 (hardback)
13 digit ISBN 978 0 431 01383 1 (hardback)
10 09 08 07 06
10 9 8 7 6 5 4 3 2 1
10 digit ISBN 0 431 01387 X (paperback)
13 digit ISBN 978 0 431 01387 9 (paperback)
11 10 09 08 07
10 9 8 7 6 5 4 3 2 1

British Library Cataloguing in Publication Data
Dalton, Dave
Environmental Migrants
  (People on the Move)
  304.8'1

A full catalogue record for this book is available from the British Library.

Acknowledgements
The publishers would like to thank the following for permission to reproduce photographs:
Associated Press p.10; Corbis pp.5, 7, 16, 30, 32, 38, 42, p.6(Lester Kefkowitz), p.9(Roger Ressmeyer), p.13(Richard Cummins), pp.14, 29(Bettmann), p.20/21(Steve Kaufman), p.32(Les Stone), p.37(Reutrers); Digital Vision p.36; Getty Images/photodisc pp.22, 40; Panos p. 25(Giacomo Pirozzi), p.34(Paul Harrison), p.45(Dean Sewell); Science Photo Library p.24; Still Pictures pp.19, 27.

Cover photograph of people fleeing from the 1984 eruption of the Mayon volcano in the Philippines, reproduced with permission of Getty Images .

The publishers would like to thank Angus Willson, Director, Worldaware for his assistance in the preparation of this book.

Every effort has been made to contact copyright holders of any material reproduced in this book. Any omissions will be rectified in subsequent printings if notice is given to the publishers.

Contents

Words appearing in bold, **like this,** are explained in the glossary.

chapter one

Introduction

The environment and people

This book is about the connections between the **environment** and **migration**. Migration is the movement of people, especially in large numbers, and usually for ever. There are many reasons for migration. Sometimes it is caused by environmental change.

The environment

Your environment is everything around you. It is the buildings, land, water, air, living things, and other people. One way to look at the environment is as a set of resources for us to use. The environment provides us with everything we need, from the air we breathe to the soil to grow food in. People have adapted to survive in even the harshest environments. The environment may look solid and settled, but it is always changing. Natural environments change very slowly if untouched by people. **Geological** change can take millions of years. When people settle in an area they often cause changes to their environment.

Cause and effect

There is a two-way relationship between people and the environment. The environment affects us, but we also affect it. We adapt to the climate and resources of the places where we live. We suit our clothing, homes and other buildings, the crops we grow, and the ways we make a living, to fit in with our environment. We make ourselves comfortable and settle down. But sometimes, as we will see in this book, the environment changes in ways that threaten people and they are driven out.

All human activity has an impact on the environment. The people with the simplest way of life are **hunter-gatherers**. They hunt animals, catch fish, and gather plant foods. Even hunter-gatherers have some effect on the environment. They take food that would otherwise be eaten by an animal. They chop down trees to burn for warmth and cooking, and to make

Before this house near the US Teton Mountains was abandoned, it gave shelter to its owners in this remote and mountainous area. This is just one example of how people have adapted to extreme and harsh environments all over the world.

temporary shelters. Most ways of life are a lot more complicated and have a lot more impact. Some activities deliberately change the environment, for instance clearing land for farming. Some change the environment without meaning to, for example increasing the **erosion** of soil by removing trees.

Consider this: your personal environment

Look around you, at home, your neighbourhood. How much of what you see is natural, and how much is artificial? How much have the natural parts been altered, or even created, by human activity? And what changes are happening to your local environment?

Finding new environments

Early humans first lived in the areas of Africa where the environment provided enough resources. Then they moved on to the rest of the world. This was a long, slow migration. People had to walk, because they had no other form of transport. They probably moved on only when their numbers became more than the local resources could support. During the **Ice Ages**, the sea level was lower than it is today. People were able to walk between places that are now separated by water. For example, they walked from Asia into North America across what is now the Bering Strait.

During the Ice Ages, most of Africa was quite a comfortable environment. It did not have cold winters. In most places, there was enough rain for plants and animals to survive. As the early humans spread out from Africa, they found different and challenging environments. Adapting to these new environments made people create new ways of life. This has led to the huge range of cultures, languages, and even appearance that the human race has today.

Why people migrate

When we talk about migrants, we do not mean individual travellers, explorers, and adventurers. Migrants move in large numbers, sometimes by the million. Very often whole families move together, or the wage earners go first and their families join them later. And most **migration** is permanent. Once they have arrived, the people stay in their destination.

Push and pull factors

To migrate causes such an upheaval that people do not do it on a whim. They have good, sometimes urgent, reasons to make a move. Most migrants move because of a mixture of push and pull factors. There are problems about staying where they are that 'push' them away. There are attractions about the places they go to that 'pull' them there. Sometimes the push factor is the stronger force, sometimes the pull factor is stronger.

There are many push and pull factors, but this book concentrates on factors linked to the **environment**. Environmental change can create push or pull factors. Natural disasters, such as volcanic eruptions, are push factors, although they may create only temporary migration. When the disaster is over, the migrants often return home.

Damming a river and creating a lake is an obvious way in which we change the environment. We can also change it in slower, more subtle ways.

Consider this:
up to you

Imagine it is your decision. Would you be tempted to stay put, hoping that things would get better? Would you feel excited about the possible new life, or nervous? Would you move a short distance, or would you be prepared to cross the world?

Find out how eating potatoes changed the environment and caused a great migration (see page 30).

Migrants cause environmental change

Sometimes people cause environmental change by their migration. When large numbers of people arrive in an area that was only thinly populated, they have a lot more impact on the environment. They can change that environment very quickly. They exploit its resources to meet their needs. When British settlers arrived in Australia at the end of the 18th century, they pushed aside the Aboriginal People, and wild animals such as kangaroos, to make way for their farms. They also brought in new crops, such as wheat and sugar cane, and new animals such as sheep.

Occasionally people damage their environment so badly that they have to leave the area. People have caused environmental change, which in turn causes migration.

The decision

Push and pull factors are real, but people are not helplessly pushed and pulled. They usually make decisions about whether to move and when, and to where. Their decisions depend on how they feel about the push and pull factors. They have to believe that their lives will be better somewhere else, although they cannot know what the future will bring. They are much more likely to migrate if they think a different environment will be significantly better than the one they are in.

Sometimes people do not have a choice. Their situation may be so catastrophic that they have to leave immediately to stay alive. They may have no idea of where they are going, or what they will do when they get there.

chapter two:

Natural disasters

Volcanoes and earthquakes

The most dramatic and sudden **environmental** changes are volcanic eruptions and earthquakes. The threat of such a catastrophe is enough to make everyone flee, even if they have no idea where they will go or how they will survive there. But very often there is no warning that these disasters are coming.

Earthquakes

An earthquake is a tremor or vibration of the Earth's **crust**. As many as 500,000 earthquakes happen every year. Up to 100 of these are violent enough to damage buildings and cause death and injury. Every few years there is one big enough to kill thousands of people.

On 26 December 2004 there was a violent earthquake on the sea bed of the Indian Ocean near Sumatra, Indonesia. It caused a huge wave, called a **tsunami,** which killed more than 200,000 people on the coasts of Indonesia, Sri Lanka, India and Thailand. Up to five million people in these countries lost their homes and livelihoods. There have been many earthquakes in the last century, when the record number of deaths was at Tangshan, China, in 1976. More than a quarter of a million people were killed.

Why, then, do people live in places where they know that earthquakes happen? Why do the survivors stay and rebuild after earthquakes? Earthquake zones occupy a large proportion of the Earth's surface. They are all around the Pacific Ocean, and in a line from China to the Mediterranean Sea. Some parts are thinly populated. Other parts are some of the most densely settled places in the world, such as India, China, Japan, Indonesia, and California in the USA. Apart from the risk of earthquakes, these are good environments in which to live. They can also support large numbers of people. Finally, earthquakes are unpredictable. People living in earthquake zones feel an earthquake may not happen soon, or ever. For all these reasons, people are prepared to take the risk. Few people **migrate** because of the threat of earthquakes.

Volcanoes

The effects of volcanic eruptions depend on the type of volcano. There may be clouds of hot or poisonous gases, flows of lava, and ash and dust blown into the sky that later settle on the land. Volcanic eruptions near the sea can also cause tidal waves (tsunamis), that destroy

After the terrible earthquake and fire that hit San Francisco in 1906, the people returned and rebuilt the city. They stayed on again after another earthquake hit the city in 1989.

coastal communities. If the eruption melts snow and ice on the summit of the volcano, this can cause floods.

When volcanoes erupt, they destroy crops and buildings, and kill people. But volcanic disasters are less frequent, and less damaging to human life, than earthquakes. People who live near a volcano often recognise signs that an eruption is about to happen. For example they feel rumbles in the ground, or see small eruptions before a big one. Scientists who study volcanoes can also warn them that an eruption is likely.

If there is warning in good time, people will flee to a safe place. This is a migration caused by environmental change. How permanent their migration is depends on how long the eruption lasts. The soils around volcanoes are **fertile**, so people like to settle on the slopes where they can grow good crops. Once the eruption is over, people are tempted to return. Up to 500 million people live near volcanoes.

Consider this:
fleeing an eruption

If you lived near a volcano, how ready would you be to leave if it showed signs of erupting? And if it did erupt, how would you feel about returning home afterwards?

case study:

Mount Pinatubo, Philippines

The Philippines is a country made up of a group of islands in the Pacific Ocean. Mount Pinatubo is one of many volcanoes there. Until 1991 Pinatubo had not erupted for 460 years. It stood 1745 metres (5725 feet) high. More than 30,000 people lived in small villages on its slopes. About 500,000 people lived in cities and villages on slopes surrounding the volcano. The Philippines is a poor country, but people living around the volcano supported themselves by farming the rich soil. In June 1991, without any warning, an explosive eruption blew almost 150 metres (500 feet) off the top of the mountain. A hole covering 5 square kilometres (2 square miles) was left in its place.

Millions of tonnes of ash fell on the land around the volcano. More than 300 people died during the eruption. Most of them died when roofs collapsed under the weight of this ash. Thousands of farmers saw their crops and homes disappear under a blanket of ash. One million farm animals died, and 200,000 homes were destroyed.

Mud and water

The troubles of the people around Pinatubo were not over. When it rained, the loose ash turned into a river of mud. Thousands of people fled from this mudslide. When they returned a few days later, they found their homes and fields ruined by the mud. Over the next ten years, the hole in the top of the volcano filled with water. It held about 210 million cubic metres (45.5 billion gallons) of water. People feared that the side of the mountain could collapse, causing a devastating flood. About 40,000 people were **evacuated**, until an escape channel for the water could be dug. The channel successfully drained off 24 million cubic metres (5.2 billion gallons) of water. People were then able to return to their homes. The western wall of the crater did collapse in 2002, slowly releasing about 160 million cubic metres (34.7 billion gallons) of water and mud, but with no harm to people.

Soon after Mount Pinatubo erupted in 1991, heavy rains turned the volcanic ash to mud.

Mount Pinatubo is on Luzon, one of the islands of the Philippines, and near the capital, Manila.

"The eruption started at 11.00 p.m. and by 12.00 it had started raining sand and ash. It sounded like thunder and lightning. You couldn't see anything at all for 24 hours. There were earthquakes and constant tremors here for a week. We stayed inside our house. We couldn't leave, there was so much ash, as Pinatubo is only 30 kilometres (18.6 miles) away. We were all very lucky that the mountain range sits between Mount Pinatubo and us. We were terrified for our children. The men would sweep the ash off the roofs to stop our houses collapsing.

It was dreadful here after the eruption. No one could earn a living. We thought of moving, but we had nowhere to go. You couldn't see anything green, everything was ash ... We had to sell our livestock because there was no food. For almost a year we survived on relief goods provided by government agencies and local donors. We survived on canned goods, dried fish, rice and noodles."

Marlyn Calderon survived the eruption. This is how she described it.

Consider this:
risk-takers

The story of Mount Pinatubo is an example of the risks people are prepared to take. The risk of the volcano erupting is a push factor. People's homes and livelihoods were destroyed by the volcano. More importantly, their lives were in such danger that they had to flee. Yet they returned and rebuilt. The pull factors meant that people did not migrate.

Drought

All life on Earth depends on water. Some plants and animals are well adapted to the very dry conditions in deserts, but human beings can never go far from a source of water. Farmers are vulnerable to **drought** because their crops need water. Without enough rain, at the right season, there will be a poor crop or none at all. Farm animals too need water and food. Without rain to make the grass grow, or to grow food for them, they will die.

Dry years

Everywhere in the world, rainfall varies from day to day, and from year to year. Many areas of the world, mainly in the **tropics**, have wet and dry seasons. Not only is there a long dry season every year, but the average rainfall over many years is low. And worse still, there are big changes between one year and another. Farmers in these areas have found ways to adapt to unreliable weather. They store grain and build up their herds in good years, so they have enough to eat in the bad years. Farmers' survival depends on them having enough seed to sow next year's crop, and enough animals to breed another flock or herd.

Drought and famine

The pattern of rainfall in places where rainfall is unreliable also varies on a longer cycle. There are not only good years and bad years, but good decades and bad decades. When there are too many bad years in a row or close together, farmers cannot build up their reserves. Worse still, they may have to eat their seed corn and their last breeding animals. Now they will have no crop and no herd next year, whatever the weather. A series of droughts can cause famine. There is nothing left but to **migrate**, to find food.

Las Vegas is in the desert in Nevada, USA. The city's growth was made possible by damming the Colorado River to create an artificial lake. This supplies water to the city.

The situation is not always this drastic, or this simple. Some people will start to leave before others. They will survive somehow until the good rains come and they can return to start again. Others will manage somehow, preserving just enough seed and a couple of animals so that they can rebuild when the good rains start. Older people, who have lived through previous droughts, can see the pattern of dry years and advise the community about the best strategy.

Irrigation

To protect themselves against drought, people **irrigate** their land. They find ways to get water from more reliable sources, such as rivers and lakes. They channel this water to their crops. They dig wells deep enough to reach water even in the driest years. They also dam rivers to create lakes. This means water can be stored in wet years, to be available in dry years.

People also find that they can use irrigation to grow crops on land that would otherwise be too dry to grow anything. For example, a series of dams across the Colorado River in the south-west of the USA provides water that enables people to live and farm in the deserts of Arizona and Nevada.

case study:

The Dust Bowl

When **drought** struck the Great Plains of the USA in the 1930s, it caused a huge **migration**. The region had already seen 60 years of **environmental** change and migration.

From Native Americans to farmers

In the early 19th century there were about 60 million American bison, or buffalo, on the Great Plains. They supported a population of 400,000 Native Americans. After the first railway crossed the plains in 1869, people could migrate more easily from the east. White settlers began to arrive. Hunters, armed with rifles, shot the buffalo for their skins. With the loss of the buffalo, and the arrival of settlers, the way of life of the Native Americans came to an end. They were moved on to **reservations**. The buffalo were replaced by herds of cattle. The Great Plains became cowboy country.

Then came farmers, who ploughed up the land to grow crops. Forty million acres of grass on the Great Plains were ploughed up, over 40 years. The migrants caused a huge and very rapid change in the environment. The tough grasses, and the buffalo that grazed them, had been well adapted to the climate. The settlers replaced them with crops and animals from outside the region. They arrived at a time of above-average rainfall, but even then the rain was unreliable. In bad years the crops failed.

Consider this: drought, or the wrong sort of farming?

The Dust Bowl might seem to be a natural disaster caused by drought. But the drought only became an environmental disaster because of people. Migration into the region caused the environmental change that created the Dust Bowl. Farmers did not realise how badly they were damaging the environment, by ploughing up the thin soils.

Dust storms like this one of 1937 destroyed farmers' livelihoods.

Drought and disaster

In the 1930s there was a run of dry years. The crops died. With no roots to hold the dry, dusty soil, the wind took it away. In April 1934, a giant black dust cloud blew over the dry and empty fields of eastern Colorado and western Kansas. The cloud was 390,000 square kilometres (627,000 square miles) in size, and contained 350 million tonnes of topsoil. It left dust drifts up to 2 metres (6 feet) deep against the sides of houses. Throughout 1934 and the first half of 1935, dust storms raged. The 'Dust Bowl' affected more than 15 per cent of the land in the USA. Land was lost in nineteen states. Fourteen million hectares of arable land were destroyed, and 90 million hectares were damaged. One billion (thousand million) tonnes of topsoil was blown away. In all, 750,000 farmers lost everything and were forced to leave their homes. Most of them went to California. Many found low-paid temporary work picking fruit and vegetables. The state of Oklahoma lost almost 20 per cent of its population.

Adapting to a harsh environment

Most people stayed on. They used better farming practices, and benefited from higher rainfall in later years. But the pattern of droughts has continued. The average rainfall per year is 50 centimetres (20 inches). This is barely enough even if it were reliable. Many farmers now rely on **irrigation**, using underground water reserves. Today fewer people live on the Great Plains than when the Native Americans lived there 150 years ago.

State	Population loss in the 1930s
Kansas	79,971
Nebraska	62,129
North Dakota	38,910
South Dakota	49,888
Oklahoma	59,606

This map shows the area of the Dust Bowl. Thousands of farmers left the region for California.

Floods

Floods can happen when rain falls more heavily than usual. They are most likely to happen when there is a lot of heavy rain in a short time. This is because there is more water than the ground can soak up, or the rivers can take away. Fast-melting snow can have the same effect. But floods are rarely a push factor that causes people to **migrate**.

Devastation

Floods destroy everything in their path, and can drown people and animals. Flash floods take people by surprise. On 15 August 1952, 23 centimetres (9 inches) of rain fell in 24 hours on Exmoor, Devon in the UK. This was too much water for the ground and rivers to soak up. Ninety million tonnes of water surged down the East and West Lyn rivers. The flood destroyed the village of Lynmouth, and killed 34 people.

In recent years, there have been heavy floods in river valleys and low-lying areas in the UK.

Coping with floods

Usually people have a warning that a flood is likely to happen and have time to prepare. This does not often mean leaving the area. Bad as floods are, they are usually over quickly. People move to higher ground, or even just to upstairs rooms in their houses. In low-lying and riverside areas, floods happen often enough for people to be used to them. Why do they stay? People stay because of the pull factors. Land that is vulnerable to floods is also usually good for crops. It is less likely to suffer **drought**. Cities often grow up beside rivers, which are useful transport routes. The push factor of floods is not as strong as the pull factor of the economic advantages of living near a river.

Protection from floods

In many places where floods occur, people have built high **embankments** to enclose rivers. However, these may just push the flood water further downstream. Over time, slow rivers drop **sediment** on their beds, causing the river level gradually to rise. The embankments then have to be raised. Another way to manage floods is to keep some areas of land clear of buildings and crops. This land can be flooded in a controlled way. The land floods but little damage is done.

Consider this:
staying put

Natural disasters do not always cause people to move away permanently. Areas that are likely to flood are often good environments. People want to live there. They try to tame nature. Many will put up with occasional floods rather than be driven away.

The Mississippi floods

In 1993, the Mississippi River Basin in the USA suffered severe floods. The area had a very wet spring. This was followed by the wettest June and July since 1895. By mid-July the Mississippi was 18 metres (59 feet) above its normal height. Embankments and dams burst. The river became 25 kilometres (15.5 miles) wide. Floodwater stretched from Memphis in the south to Minneapolis in the north. It covered 23 million acres, an area greater than Britain. Nine states were affected. Almost 70,000 people were **evacuated** from their homes, and 48 people died. The flood disrupted transport and caused an estimated $10 billion (thousand million) of damage. People quickly returned and rebuilt after the flood. The rich soils and cheap water transport make the Mississippi River valley a good place to live.

The Mississippi floods of 1993 left only the tops of buildings showing.

Bangladesh

Bangladesh is a country in Asia next to India. Most of it lies around the **delta** of the Ganges and Brahmaputra rivers. The land is mainly low-lying. The delta floods every year, when the snows of the Himalayan mountains melt and the **monsoon** rains fall. The people of Bangladesh value this flooding because it deposits another layer of **silt** in the fields. This silt makes the land more **fertile**. The floodwater is essential to growing paddy rice. The combination of tropical climate, plenty of water, and fertile soil means that good crops can be grown. Bangladesh has a population of over 141 million, in an area of 144,000 square kilometres (89,500 square miles), slightly larger than the US state of Louisiana. This makes it the most densely populated country in the world.

Floods

Floods are essential to life in Bangladesh, but they can also cause damage. Most people's homes are built of bamboo and thatch. A higher flood than usual can wash houses away. If the floodwater stays too long, crops will be damaged or washed away. Then the landless labourers will have no work and no wages, so people will go hungry. And in the worst floods, people are drowned. More people die of disease, because they have had to drink polluted water.

In 1998, Bangladesh suffered from the worst flood on record. The flood lasted for three months. Two-thirds of the country was under water. Hundreds of people died. Around 30 million people were affected. The floods destroyed half a million tonnes of rice, and prevented farmers from planting dry-season rice. Ten million people were out of work. Most of them had no savings, and relied on each day's work to buy food for their families.

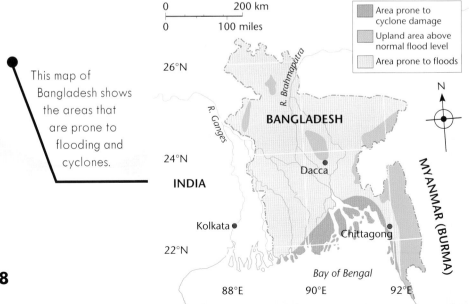

This map of Bangladesh shows the areas that are prone to flooding and cyclones.

During floods people have to use boats or wade through the flood water.

Internal migration

Most people in Bangladesh are poor. They have no savings, and rely on what they can grow, or on work in other people's fields. So they are much more vulnerable to the effects of flooding that make farming impossible. The poorest people are those who have no land. They settle on islands of silt that appear when the rivers change course. This is an internal **migration,** in which the push factor is poverty. The pull factor is the new, free land of the silt islands. These islands are the most vulnerable to damaging flooding.

Cyclones

Cyclones are violent tropical storms. When a cyclone hits Bangladesh, there is nothing to slow down the wind because the land is so flat. The cyclone destroys everything in its path. The storm coming in from the Bay of Bengal pushes the sea in front of it in a huge wave. The surge of seawater takes people by surprise. On 29 April 1991, the worst cyclone of the century struck Bangladesh. Winds of 233 kilometres (145 miles) per hour caused a storm surge of 6 metres (20 feet). Over 139,000 people were killed and 10 million people lost their homes.

Consider this:
floods, cyclones, or poverty?

Many Bangladeshis have migrated permanently to countries such as Britain. Many more have migrated temporarily to jobs in the Gulf States. Others have migrated from the countryside in Bangladesh to the cities. The push factors behind these migrations include the danger of floods and cyclones. Many people are also escaping the poverty that makes them so vulnerable to floods and cyclones. Which is the greatest push factor? Floods, cyclones, or poverty?

Chapter three

Human causes

Farming and over-farming

Hunter-gatherers had little impact on their **environment**. It was only when people became farmers that they started to affect it. The impact of farming on the environment has increased over time, up to the present day. Farming and over-farming often cause **migration**.

Farmers try to control and change the environment. The fields contain only the plants, called crops, that the farmer wants to grow there. All other plants are weeds, which the farmer tries to get rid of. In the same way, a farmer only wants to keep useful animals, which provide meat, milk, eggs, or wool. All other animals are treated as pests.

Farmers and migrants

Farming produced so much more food from the land than hunter-gathering. This meant that the population was able to grow quickly. The surplus people migrated to look for new land to farm. This second long, slow, uncounted migration gradually filled all the parts of the world that could be farmed. The push factor was population growth, which meant not enough land for everyone to farm. The pull factor was an environment which could be exploited.

This Russian whaling village and processing factory has been abandoned. Most countries stopped catching whales in the 1980s, to prevent whales being wiped out.

Consider this: over-fishing

Worldwide, about 1 billion people rely on fish and other seafood as their main source of animal protein. Each year, about 80 million tonnes of wild fish are caught in the world's oceans. With modern fishing methods, it is very easy to catch fish faster than they can breed. At least 10 per cent of the world's sea-fish populations are over-fished. The only solution is to catch fewer fish, but that is bad for communities which rely on fishing. People there may leave to find work elsewhere, in a migration pushed by environmental change.

Selective breeding and more migrants

Farmers also worked on getting more food out of their land. They saved the ears of wheat with the most grains to sow in the next season, so gradually crop yields improved. They bred from the cows that gave the most milk, so gradually milk yields improved. This selective breeding meant more food, which soon meant more people. When people ran out of land to farm, they started another kind of migration. They began to clear land for farming in areas they had previously avoided, such as forests, swamps, and hillsides.

More developments

As farming developed, new practices such as selective breeding and the use of better machinery and chemicals, increased the impact on the environment. The more a farm concentrates on just one crop, or type of animal, the more it is at risk from frost, **drought**, flood, pests, and diseases. And the bigger the population relying on that crop, the more they are at risk if the crop fails.

Over-cropping and over-grazing

Farming can damage the environment on which it depends. Growing the same crop every year uses up the nutrients in the soil. The crop will not grow well if it cannot get these nutrients. This is called over-cropping. Grazing animals on the same land, without giving the plants time to grow back, is called over-grazing. It is also harmful. It removes the plants which keep the soil in place. Without this ground cover, the soil is **eroded** away. At its worst, over-farming can lead to a collapse of farming. People have to migrate away from the area, as there is no food supply.

Collapsing civilizations

In the rainforests of the Yucatan peninsula shared by Mexico, Belize, and Guatemala, there are mysterious ruins. They include pyramids, temples, huge carved heads, and inscriptions. Experts who have studied these ruins think that there were towns with tens of thousands of people living in them. These civilizations had writing, religion, astronomy, and calendars. The civilizations were all supported by farming. What happened to them?

The Olmecs and the Maya

The Olmec civilization flourished between 800 and 400 BC. Its most unusual remains are huge carved heads. These are 2.5 metres (9 feet) tall. They were made from **basalt** rock that had been transported from quarries over 100 kilometres (62 miles) away.

The Maya civilization existed between AD 300 and 900. It left even more impressive traces, such as pyramids that are 58 metres (190 feet) high. Its cities had up to 40,000 inhabitants. These cities could only have existed if the farming nearby was efficient enough to produce food for everyone. There may have been as many as 250 people living in each square kilometre (0.4 square miles). This is similar to many countries in modern Europe. The population of the Maya region at its peak might have been 5 million. Today the area supports only a few tens of thousands. Where did the people go? It is impossible to be sure what happened, but experts agree that one of the factors was an **environmental** disaster caused by over-farming.

The Maya built pyramids and temples, and had a written script and astronomy. The collapse of their civilization may have been caused by the destruction of their environment.

The ruins of Maya cities are in the Yucatan region of Mexico, Belize, and Guatemala.

The disaster

The Maya civilization was based on **intensive agriculture**. They cleared forests and made terraces on the hillsides. They also drained the swampy lowlands. They wanted as much land as possible for growing crops, such as maize, beans, cotton, and cacao. In the tropical climate they could grow good crops. But the soil began to lose its **fertility**, as crops were taken from it year after year. As the population increased, there may have been pressure to extend farming further into the forest. The soil, once cleared of its forest cover, was easily **eroded**. Heavy rainfall took the soil away from the hillside fields. At the same time, the soil filled the **drainage ditches** in the lowlands. When crop yields fell, people tried to farm on even steeper slopes, creating yet more erosion.

Skeletons found in burials from about AD 800 show signs of disease caused by shortage of food. Food shortages could have caused cities to fight each other over land. These wars added to the hunger and disease. This probably tipped the Maya civilization over the edge, into collapse. Before long, rainforest covered the deserted cities.

Consider this: choices

Sometimes when people destroy their environment, they may feel that they have no choice. They may think it is better to grow some food this year than to go hungry. This may have been the case with the Mayans. The combination of a growing population, intensive farming, and a fragile environment has existed in many other places. It still exists today.

Trees and soil

Many parts of the world would naturally be covered in a thick forest of large trees, if they were not currently being farmed. In the UK, for example, oak and ash forest would grow back within 150 years on the land that is farmed today, if it was left alone. It is impossible to farm in a forest, the trees must be cut down. But in some places, destroying forests damages the **environment** so badly that people have to move away.

Useful trees

When people cut down trees, they gain not only land but also timber for building, and firewood. Trees have many other uses if they are not cut down. They provide food for animals, and many have medical uses. So even in the most **intensively farmed** places, people have kept trees around their homes and villages.

Soil

In some parts of the world, such as most of northern Europe, the soil in woods is **fertile**. It provides good crops after the trees have been cleared. The weather is never so dry that the soil turns to dust and blows away, or so wet that it washes away. Other parts of the world, especially in the **tropics**, are less fortunate. Once the trees are gone, the soil is easily **eroded** by the weather. After a few years of growing crops, the soil is so infertile that the land is no good for farming. If it is used for grazing animals, the animals will eat the shoots of any trees that start to grow. The forest can never regrow.

The roots of trees absorb a lot of rain. They also slow down the water that passes through the soil to the rock below. When the trees are gone, heavy rainfall in the wet season causes floods. In the dry season, wells and springs dry up without the slow release of water from the soil.

Local people know the long-term value of the forest. But if they are desperately poor they may feel they have no choice. They must exploit the environment just to survive. Eventually, without soil for their crops, and with floods in the wet season and **drought** in the dry season, they may be forced to **migrate** away.

This hillside in Nepal has been badly eroded, because the trees that used to grow here were cut down.

Reforestation

Sometimes people manage to stop the destruction. The people of the village of Kesharpur in Orissa, India, saw the forest on the hill above their village being destroyed. They formed an organization with 21 other villages around the hill. They agreed to take action to stop the destruction, and to reforest the hill. The organization put strict controls on sheep and goats, which eat tree seedlings and prevent regrowth. This was a difficult decision for poor people, whose sheep and goats may have been their only source of income. The villagers managed to bring the forest back to life. Within a few years the forest started to regrow, the wildlife returned, and the springs began to flow again.

A family in Mali, Africa, watering tree seedlings.

Consider this:
a worthwhile sacrifice

All over the poor countries of the world, people recognise the problem of deforestation and want to replant their forests. But like the villagers of Kesharpur, they may have to make hard sacrifices now, to give the forest a future.

Case study:

Amazonia

The last great areas of uncleared forest are the tropical rainforests. The largest area of tropical rainforest is Amazonia, in South America. Until the 1960s there were not many people living there. There were only some **hunter-gatherer** peoples, and some settlers who tapped the rubber trees and collected brazil nuts. Then in the 1970s the government of Brazil started to build roads through the rainforest. This opened the forest up to settlers, ranchers, and loggers. Prospectors came looking for gold, iron, manganese, and aluminium. **Geologists** came looking for oil. Amazonia is the scene of one of today's biggest **migrations**.

Settlers and clearance

The government of Brazil wanted to encourage people to move away from the north-east of the country, where **drought** had made the land very poor. Their plan worked. For example, the territory of Rondonia was opened up by a road from Cuiabá to Porto Velho. As a result of migration, the population increased from 113,000 to 1.09 million between 1970 and 1990. In some areas, the population doubled every two years.

Fragile forest

A tropical rainforest depends on the recycling of its plants. Living plants grow in the decomposed remains of dead plants. There may be only 2.5–5 centimetres (1–2 inches) of topsoil in a tropical rainforest. Once a rainforest has been cleared, the soil can only support farming for a year or two. The soil is **eroded**, so the settlers and ranchers give up and move on to newly cleared areas. The abandoned land will probably recover eventually, but the clearance is so recent that no-one knows how long that recovery will take. And it may never again be as lush as the original rainforest.

The Transansamazônica and other new roads have opened Amazonia up to settlers, prospectors, ranchers, and loggers.

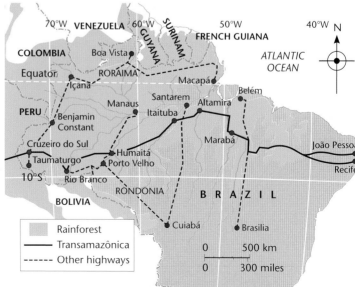

The people of the forest

The **indigenous people** of the forest are not only threatened by the clearance of the land. They have lived for thousands of years without contact with other people. When settlers come, the indigenous people are in danger of catching diseases that they have never been exposed to before. Even childhood illnesses among the settlers, such as measles, can be fatal for the indigenous people.

The pressures

Despite all these problems, the clearance and migration continue. Poor, landless people from elsewhere in Brazil are desperate for land on which to farm. The other pressure on the forest comes from rich people who plan to make money from logging, ranching, or mining. These people will not suffer from the consequences of deforestation because they do not need to live in Amazonia. Similar combinations of clearing, migration, and exploitation are affecting other rainforests, such as those in Indonesia.

New roads cut straight through the forest allow migrants to settle in Amazonia.

Roraima

In 1978, the Brazilian state of Roraima had 80,000 inhabitants. Of these, 32,000 were Amazonian Indians. About 70 per cent of the area was forested. By 1996, the population had grown to 262,000. All this growth was made up of migrants. The push factor for these migrants was poverty. The pull factor was the promise of a better life. The newcomers in Roraima used fire and bulldozers to clear the forest. A hectare (2.5 acres) of cleared land in Roraima is worth ten times more than a hectare of forest.

Famine

In a famine thousands, or sometimes millions, of people die of hunger because of a shortage of food. The shortage may be caused by **drought**, or by a crop disease that destroys the harvest. But that is not the whole story. Why cannot food be brought to the hungry people? Why did people in the USA not go hungry when the Mississippi River floods of 1993 destroyed 2.5 million hectares (6 million acres) of food crops? Why cannot the hungry people **migrate** to where there is food?

Help

Poverty is the main factor behind famine. After a crop failure, the price of food rises to a level people cannot afford to pay. We expect governments to help people when there is famine, and of course they do. An international organization, the World Food Programme, also supplies food to countries suffering from food shortages. Other non-government organizations and charities also help with aid. But sometimes the government has other priorities. Sometimes famines are made worse by the wars affecting the country. In poor countries, the people who are not starving may have just enough to survive. They may have nothing to give those who are starving.

Staying put

So why do people not migrate to where there is food? Sometimes the famine affects such a wide area that there is nowhere to go. The starving people have nothing with which to buy food. If they do set off in search of food, they may not reach the supplies in time. Sometimes they are prevented from getting away from the famine area by wars.

Part of Ethiopia is in the Sahel, a drought-prone region that lies between the Sahara to the north, and the more fertile area to the south.

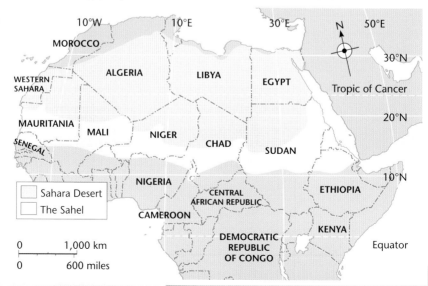

10°W   10°E   30°E   N   50°E

MOROCCO

30°N

WESTERN SAHARA

ALGERIA   LIBYA   EGYPT

Tropic of Cancer

20°N

MAURITANIA   MALI   NIGER   CHAD   SUDAN

SENEGAL

☐ Sahara Desert
☐ The Sahel

NIGERIA

10°N

CENTRAL AFRICAN REPUBLIC

ETHIOPIA

CAMEROON

KENYA

0   1,000 km
0   600 miles

DEMOCRATIC REPUBLIC OF CONGO

Equator

Consider this:
why stay?

Why do people stay in a country that is prone to drought and famine? Where would they go? They would not be welcome, or find things much better, in the countries neighbouring Ethiopia. These countries are also poor and drought-prone. And it's hard for poor people from a country like Ethiopia to reach, or to be allowed to enter, a rich country.

Ethiopia 1984

Ethiopia is one of many poor African countries with low and unreliable rainfall. Between 1972 and 1974 famine killed 200,000 people. The harvests of the next few years were barely enough to feed the population. Meanwhile, war had broken out between the government and the region of Eritrea, which wanted independence. Severe drought struck again over most of the country in 1983 and 1984. It tipped millions of people over the edge into famine. Millions left their villages to go to relief camps, in a huge short-term migration. They travelled on foot, over mountains, for days. The crowded and unhygienic camps created the perfect conditions for disease to break out. And there was not enough food, even in the camps. There were no food reserves in the country. International donors were slow to provide the quantity of food that was needed. Up to 1 million people died of hunger and disease in Ethiopia between 1983 and 1985. When the relief operation finally got going properly, and food reached the camps and villages it saved up to 7 million lives.

A family in the Kassala relief camp, Sudan, in 1984. They had fled famine and civil war in Ethiopia.

case study:

The Irish Potato Famine

In 1846 there were 8.5 million people living in Ireland. There were 650,000 landless labourers. Potatoes were grown in nearly 40 per cent of the crop area. Potatoes were the only food for nearly half the population. The potato, which had been introduced from South America, was vulnerable to bad weather and disease. Crop failures from 1739 to 1741 caused the deaths of half a million people.

Potato blight

In June 1845, a **fungal disease** called potato blight arrived in Ireland from the USA. Blight spreads quickly. It can wipe out the whole crop, and rot potatoes that are in storage. By August, the disease had spread all over Europe. But it was only in Ireland that so many people depended completely on potatoes. The crop failed partially in 1845, and totally in 1846. Poor people made up a third of the population. With no reserves of food or savings, these people went hungry. They had no crop of their own, and could not afford to buy food.

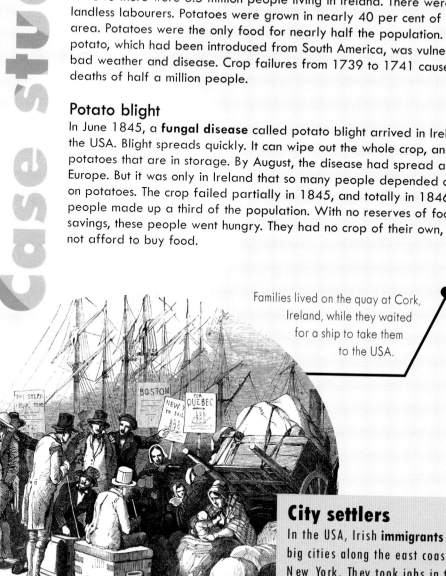

Families lived on the quay at Cork, Ireland, while they waited for a ship to take them to the USA.

City settlers

In the USA, Irish **immigrants** settled in the big cities along the east coast, such as New York. They took jobs in the police and fire services. In Britain, they worked in railway construction or joined the army. The Irish immigrants collected together in big cities, especially Glasgow and Liverpool. In 1851, 25 per cent of the population of Liverpool had been born in Ireland.

Stephen de Vere sailed from Ireland to the USA in 1847. He wrote afterwards:

Hundreds of poor people, men, women and children of all ages, huddled together without light, without air, wallowing in filth and breathing a fetid atmosphere, sick in body, dispirited in heart; the fevered patients lying beside the sound, by their agonised ravings disturbing those around. The food is generally ill-selected and seldom sufficiently cooked in consequences of the insufficiency and bad construction of the cooking places. The supply of water, hardly enough for cooking and drinking, does not allow for washing. No moral restraint is attempted; the voice of prayer is never heard; drunkenness, with all its consequent train of ruffianly debasement, is not discouraged because it is found profitable by the captain who traffics in grog [watered-down rum].

Help

Ireland was part of the United Kingdom. The government was unwilling to provide much help for the hungry people of Ireland. They believed it was wrong for governments to intervene in free trade. They allowed a large part of the Irish grain harvest to be exported. This was because the people of Ireland were too poor to pay for grain, and it could get a better price abroad. In 1846, the government provided 'relief work', such as building roads, for 500,000 people. Charities fed some of the hungry people. But the help was too little and too late to prevent famine.

Migration

About 1 million people died in Ireland, from hunger or disease. It was one of the greatest human disasters of the 19th century anywhere in the world. Another 1.6 million people **emigrated**, during or immediately after the famine. They went mainly to Britain and the USA. Desperate to flee the famine, people sold their last possessions to pay for a ticket on a crowded ship. Another 3 million people had left by the end of the 19th century. By 1900, the population of Ireland was down to 4.5 million people. Even now, its population is only about 5.4 million people. The tradition of emigration continued throughout the 20th century.

Consider this:
somewhere to go

When famine struck Ireland in the 1840s, people had somewhere to migrate to, unlike the people of Ethiopia in the 1980s. Once there was an established Irish community in the USA to welcome migrants, the move was easier to make. This added to the pull factor. People who had emigrated and done well might even pay for the tickets for their relatives to join them.

Nuclear accidents

Nuclear power stations are one way of generating electricity. They have been built all over the world. But the **radioactive** elements that power the stations are extremely dangerous. If the radioactive particles escape they spread far, damaging human health and the **environment** for many years. Nuclear accidents have caused people to **migrate**.

Chernobyl

The former Soviet Union (part of which is now known as Russia) supported nuclear power. By 1986 it had 71 nuclear power stations. One of them was at Chernobyl, near the city of Kiev, in what is now the independent country of Ukraine. On 26 April 1986, there was an explosion in one of the four reactor units of the Chernobyl station. Two people were killed in the explosion. Radioactivity was released into the air when the reactor and the surrounding protective wall blew apart. Helicopters smothered the fires with sand, and the power station was eventually buried in 300,000 cubic metres (1,094,000 cubic feet) of concrete.

Effects in the Ukraine

More than 10,000 people died as a direct result of the accident at Chernobyl. The Ukrainian government says 3.5 million people, a third of them children, became ill. Some women who were pregnant at the time of the disaster gave birth to severely disabled children. The rate of **thyroid** cancer in affected areas increased by ten times. An area 30 kilometres (18.6 miles) around the power station was declared unsafe. Sixty thousand buildings had to be **decontaminated**. **Dykes** had to be built to prevent radioactive water getting into the rivers. Even topsoil and the leaves from trees were removed and buried as nuclear waste. Kiev, a city of 2.5 million people, was near enough to Chernobyl to be badly affected.

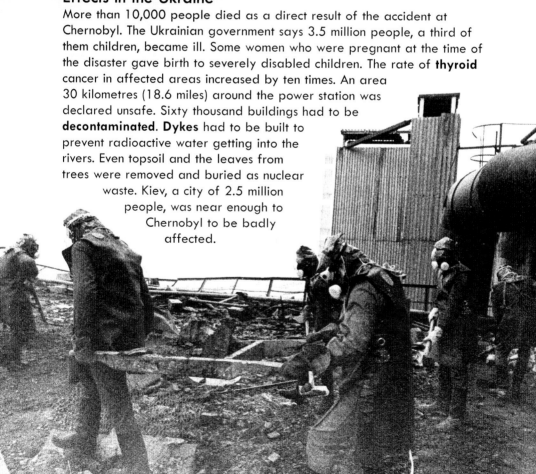

The explosion and fire at Chernobyl threw radioactive dust high into the atmosphere. The arrows show the route of the radioactive dust.

Map labels: 20°W, 0°, 20°E, 40°E, 60°E, Arctic Circle, 60°N, 40°N, N
26–29 April, Chernobyl, Kiev, 2–4 May, 30 April–1 May
0   1000 km
0   600 miles

Consider this: the cost of electricity

Chernobyl was finally closed in 2000. There are advantages and disadvantages in using nuclear power to make electricity. One disadvantage is that nuclear accidents have far-reaching effects. These benefits and costs have to be balanced against other ways of making electricity, which affect the environment in different ways.

Emergency workers remove radioactive debris after the explosion at Chernobyl.

Effects in the rest of Europe

Wind carried the radioactive dust over much of northern Europe. Rain brought the dust down on to the land, contaminating plants and animals. Reindeer in Lapland were unfit to eat. More than 4 million sheep in Wales, the Lake District, and Scotland were affected at first. The effects of the disaster are till detectable today. Some British sheep will probably be unsafe to eat for another ten to fifteen years.

Migration

The accident forced a migration in 1986. About 400,000 people had to leave their homes. The government moved them very quickly. Often they took only the few possessions they could carry. The migrants needed houses, schools, and jobs. This caused severe problems in the places they were moved to, such as overcrowded housing and schools. People who had made their living by farming had to find jobs in cities. Some of them remain unemployed. The countryside around Chernobyl is still radioactive and empty. The migrants can never go back.

chapter four

The issues

Population growth

People affect the **environment** in many ways. When the number of people increases, their impact on the environment also increases. For most of history, the population has increased slowly, limited by disease and available food supply. Over the last 200 years there have been improvements in health care. People began to live longer, and more children survived childhood. This led to a dramatic rise in population. All these people need somewhere to live and food to eat. As we have seen in previous chapters, the impact on the environment created by so many people has caused some people to **migrate** in search of a better life.

A family planning poster from Nigeria.

Faster growth

In 1825, the world's population first reached 1 billion (thousand million) people. As the table shows it grew steadily until the 20th century, when it began to grow much faster. The rate of population growth is now beginning to slow down. The big question is whether the world's population will stabilize at 8, 10, or 12 billion?

Year	Population
1825	1 billion
1925	2 billion
1960	3 billion
1975	4 billion
1987	5 billion
2002	over 6 billion

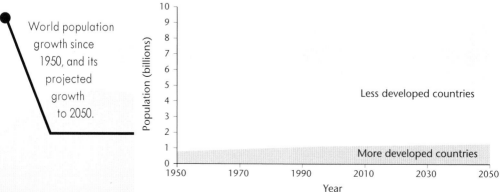

World population growth since 1950, and its projected growth to 2050.

Consider this:
people and impact

The size of the population tells only part of the story about its impact on the environment. As the table below shows, people in rich countries consume much more, and produce much more waste, than people in poor countries.

Countries	Percentage of the world's population	Percentage of the world's energy use	Amount of water used, in litres per person per day
North America, Europe, Japan, and Australasia	25	80	up to 1000
Latin America, the Caribbean, Africa, Asia, and the Middle East	75	20	20-40

Feeding the 6 billion

More people need more water, homes, jobs, fuel, and food. They also produce more waste. All this has an impact on the environment. There are two ways to grow more food. One is to farm more intensively. That means using chemical fertilizers on the soil, herbicides to kill weeds, and pesticides to kill insects and disease organisms. This may result in dangerous chemicals being released into the environment. Rain washes the chemicals into **groundwater** and rivers. People then drink this polluted water. Many people fear that over-use of chemical fertilizers also damages the soil. If the environment is very badly damaged, it cannot support the same number of people. Some people have to move away. They become environmental migrants.

The second way to grow more food is for farmers to migrate into new areas. They drain swamps, cut down forests, plough up grassland, and **irrigate** deserts. This can damage fragile environments. Farming may then have to be abandoned, and the people may have to leave. Even if the newly farmed environment is not damaged, problems can result elsewhere. One reason for the damaging floods in Bangladesh may be that people have cleared forests in the Himalayas for farming. More water runs more quickly down the hills when it rains, so people hundreds of kilometres downstream suffer from floods. They then have to migrate.

Indigenous people

The areas into which farmers migrate may be new to farming, but they are not empty. **Indigenous people** live there. The arrival of farmers forces them to migrate out of the area. Their way of life may be destroyed. In the past, settlers were quite ruthless about pushing indigenous people out of the way, but nowadays there is more concern about their rights.

Industrialization

Not only is the population bigger than ever, but more people are living in cities and working in factories. The **industrial** way of life increases our impact on the **environment**. This often causes **migration**.

Resources

Poor countries industrialize in the hope of becoming richer. Rich countries continue to grow economically. This means they need more and more raw materials such as timber, metal ores, and building materials. They also use a lot of energy from non-renewable sources, such as coal, oil, and natural gas. Individuals in rich countries also consume much more. They create a demand for products such as out-of-season foods, and luxury goods.

Collecting and transporting these raw materials and goods has a huge impact on the environment. It also affects the people who live in the places where they come from. The Grasberg mine in Irian Jaya is one of the world's largest copper and gold mines. It has devastated the local environment. For example, mining waste is pumped into the rivers. The Kamoro and Amungme people who live in the area have lost their land and livelihoods. Many of them have been forced to move away.

A global economy

Very few places in the world are isolated from the demands and impact of the rich, industrial **economies**. Some migrants to the rainforest simply grow rice and beans, and keep chickens. Others migrate there to make money by selling goods to richer countries. They may herd cattle to export for meat, cut down teak trees to export for furniture, or work in mines and oilfields.

Trees from tropical rainforests provide timber for industries in rich countries. But at the same time the **indigenous people** of the forest lose the environment on which they depend.

These people are moving out of the city of Fengjie in China, which will be submerged when the Three Gorges Dam is completed.

Dams

Building dams across rivers creates many benefits. Dams help to prevent damaging floods downstream, and even out the flow of water between seasons. The water in the lake behind the dam can be used for **irrigation**. It can also be used to generate 'clean' hydro-electricity. Not surprisingly, many dams have been built all over the world. Many poor countries see dam building as one of the ways in which they can develop.

But dams also cause problems. They hold up the **silt** which used to fertilize fields downstream. Farmers then have to use artificial fertilizers. Dams can affect fishing, and the use of the river for transport. Dams also displace people from the areas which are flooded. They become unwilling environmental migrants. The world's biggest and most controversial dam project is the Three Gorges Dam on the Yangtze River, in China. This will displace 1.9 million people. The government that is building the dam is responsible for finding homes, land, and jobs for the migrants created by the dam. What impact will these new migrants have on the places they move to?

Consider this:
levelling up – or down?

The impact on the environment of the average person in the USA is 250 times that of the average person in Africa. The only way to free up resources so that people in poor countries can escape their poverty, is for people in rich countries to consume less. What are you willing to give up?

Climate change

Environmental change can cause huge **migrations**. Many experts think that we are about to see enormous environmental disruptions caused by climate change. These disruptions may in turn cause massive migrations. In these two pages we look at the background to climate change. On pages 40–41 we will see some of the possible environmental consequences, and how these might cause migration.

Weather and climate

Just as the weather can change from day to day, so the climate can change on a longer timescale. The human race has lived through a series of **Ice Ages**. These affected the routes of the first long, slow migration out of Africa into the rest of the world. Going further back in time, scientists have found evidence of **mass extinctions**. Some of these may have been caused by sudden and drastic climate change. Living things could not adapt fast enough to the changes, so they died out.

Greenhouse gases

Scientists who study the climate say that we are in the early stages of climate change. The change has been triggered by 'greenhouse gases'. In a garden greenhouse, the glass lets sunlight in to warm the air, but prevents the warmth escaping. Greenhouse gases in the Earth's atmosphere trap heat around the Earth. The most common greenhouse gas is carbon dioxide (CO_2). There is already a small proportion of CO_2 in the atmosphere. We add to the CO_2 in the atmosphere when we cut down trees and burn wood.

Halocarbons called CFCs were used in aerosol cans, fridges, and air-conditioning units until the late 1980s. They leaked into the atmosphere, damaging the ozone layer, which protects the surface of the Earth from the dangerous **ultraviolet rays** in sunlight.

Consider this:
science, pressure, and action

The most harmful halocarbon gases came close to destroying the ozone layer, before scientists and environmentalists warned of the danger. Since the late 1980s they have been replaced by less harmful halocarbons, but it will be decades before the ozone layer repairs itself. Will the same pattern apply to greenhouse gases?

The world has warmed slowly in the last 200 years, but scientists predict that warming will happen faster in the next 100 years.

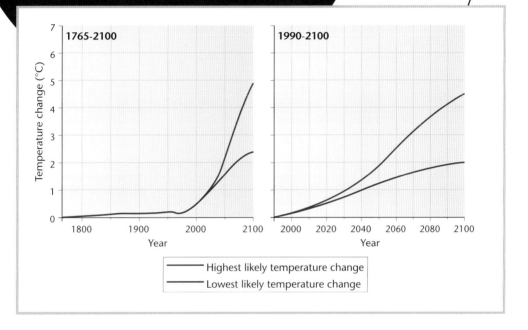

1765-2100

1990-2100

Temperature change (°C)

Year

Year

——— Highest likely temperature change
——— Lowest likely temperature change

Recent changes

However, until recently the effect was tiny. Now the proportion of CO_2 has risen fast and is still rising. This is mostly because of industrialization. Burning **fossil fuels** such as coal, oil, and natural gas, pumps millions of tonnes of CO_2 into the air. Perhaps half of it is dissolved in the oceans, leaving the rest to build up in the atmosphere.

Other greenhouse gases include methane, nitrous oxide, ozone, and halocarbons. Halocarbons are man-made gases. They are thousands of times more powerful than greenhouse gases and they can stay in the atmosphere for hundreds of years. They have been blamed for damaging the ozone layer in the atmosphere.

Global warming

Greenhouse gases in the atmosphere have begun to cause global warming. This is predicted to continue. Scientists think that the temperature on Earth will rise by 1.4–5.8 °C (2.5–10.4 °F) by 2100. How will migration be affected by the changes to the environment that global warming will bring?

The consequences of global warming

The consequences of global warming depend on whether or not we reduce the level of greenhouse gases we release. It is hard to predict exactly what the effects on the **environment** will be. As we have seen, people will put up with a lot of risks. But when things get too bad they will **migrate** in large numbers. The Irish Potato Famine of the 1840s and the Dust Bowl in the USA in the 1930s are good examples. The environmental consequences of global warming could cause huge migrations.

This island off New Caledonia in the Pacific Ocean would disappear under water if there was a significant increase in sea level.

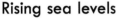

Rising sea levels

If ice sheets at the North and South Poles and the glaciers of high mountains melt they will release enormous amounts of water. One estimate is that sea levels could rise by 40 centimetres (15.8 inches) by the year 2080. At the worst, they could rise by 1 metre (3.65 feet) by 2100. Huge areas of low-lying coastal land could disappear under the sea.

This is a problem for any country with an sea coast. It is a serious problem for low-lying countries, such as Bangladesh and the Netherlands, especially if they are densely populated. Some low-lying islands, such as Tuvalu, in the Pacific Ocean, are also at risk. Worldwide, 70 million people could be affected by rising sea levels by 2100. Today about 10 million people are at risk of flooding from storm surges, such as the cyclones that affect Bangladesh (see pages 18–19). Cyclones come inland from the sea. The higher the sea level, the further the storms will reach and the more damage they will cause. By 2080, 94 million people could be at risk.

Rich countries will be able to afford to build flood defenses and warning systems to alert people of danger. Poor countries will struggle to do this. We have seen how vulnerable the Bangladeshis are to floods and cyclones. If rising sea levels make the problems worse, millions of people may migrate.

Areas of the world that would be at risk from the effects of global warming.

Consider this:
predicting the consequences

No one knows how far, or how fast, global warming will go, or its exact impact on migration. But we can be sure that global warming will be a problem for rich countries, and a disaster for poor ones. And that the migrants will come from the poor countries. Where will they go?

Drier tropics

Global warming would change the pattern of wetter and drier areas in the world. It would create a drier climate in many parts of the tropics, including Australia, India, southern Africa, and most of South America. Except for Australia, these are regions where many countries are already very poor and there is barely enough food. In the first few years of the 21st century there have already been famines caused by **drought** in Afghanistan, Ethiopia, and southern Africa. There are about 800 million malnourished people in the world. By 2080 there could be 80 million more, most of them in Africa. If drought and famine become permanent, millions may migrate to escape hunger.

Storms

If global warming increases, extreme weather, such as floods and cyclones, will become more frequent. The effects of storms are much worse in poor countries than in rich ones. If they become too frequent, millions of people in poor countries may migrate to safer places.

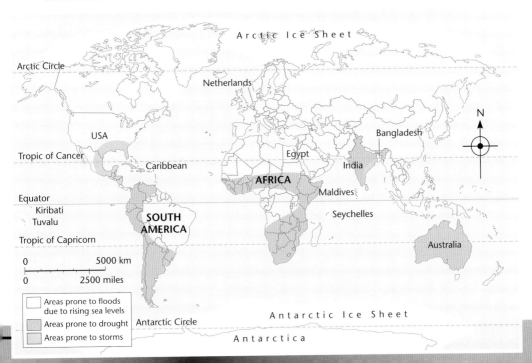

Areas prone to floods due to rising sea levels
Areas prone to drought
Areas prone to storms

Responses to global warming

Faced with the possibility of future mass **migration** due to **environmental** change, how have world leaders responded?

The Kyoto Treaty

In 1997 the leaders of the world's **industrialized** countries met in Kyoto, Japan, to discuss climate change. They agreed to reduce the worldwide release of greenhouse gases by an average of 5.2 per cent below their 1990 levels, over the next decade. A few countries, such as Britain, have met this target, but many have not. Even the target figure falls far short of the 60 or 70 per cent cuts that would be needed to make a real difference to climate change.

Reluctant reducers

In 2001 President Bush of the USA withdrew his country's commitment to the Kyoto Treaty. He said the treaty was unfair because it placed all the responsibility on rich, industrialized countries, with none for developing countries. Rich industrialized countries need to burn **fossil fuels** to maintain their prosperous lifestyles. People there expect their standard of living to continue improving.

Doubters

Some people are not convinced by the science behind global warming. The Earth's atmosphere is complicated and no one can claim to be absolutely sure about what is happening. They can be even less sure about what will happen in the future. On the other hand, most scientists agree that global warming, caused by greenhouse gases, is really happening. Even if the risk is not totally proven, it is sensible to prepare now. If we wait for final proof, it may be too late to act.

However, this will use even more energy and release even more greenhouse gases. To reduce the gases by 60 or 70 per cent would mean enormous changes in these nations' **economies**, industries, and ways of life. These changes would be as far-reaching as industrialization itself, but would have to be achieved in just a few decades.

Rich and poor
Rich countries produce much more of the greenhouse gases than poor countries, as shown in the table below.

Country	Amount of carbon produced per person per year
USA	5.99 tonnes
UK	2.1 tonnes
India	0.31 tonnes
Bangladesh	0.05 tonnes
Ethiopia	0.03 tonnes

Many of the predicted effects of global warming will hurt the poor countries worst. Rich countries will be much better able to cope with them.

A migration crisis?
Environmental change caused by global warming will push the poorest people into complete destitution. Millions of lives will be at risk from storms, flooding, **drought**, and famine. Sooner or later we must expect great migrations. People will move from areas that have become uninhabitable, to wherever they can. Very often they will reach countries that are hardly any better off.

When millions of destitute environmental migrants arrive in a country that is already poor, they may bring a crisis with them. They may force a further migration into a third country. Rich countries may eventually have to cope with millions of environmental migrants.

The things that people in rich countries take for granted, such as cars and planes, are contributing to the greenhouse effect and global warming. Can we learn to change the way we live?

Consider this: changing our world?

Environmental groups suggest ways to reduce our production of greenhouse gases. Better public transport in cities reduces the need for individual car journeys. Better-insulated buildings need less energy to heat. Electricity can be generated from the wind and the waves. All these ideas are now being put into practice in a small way, but there is still a very long way to go.

chapter five

Conclusion

Building a sustainable future

Global warming is the biggest **environmental** problem facing the world today. Some say it is the biggest single problem facing the world. And it is not the only big change in the environment that is happening. Around 15 per cent of our agricultural land has badly damaged soil. Every year 24 billion tonnes of topsoil are lost by **erosion**. The rainforests are disappearing. Farmland is disappearing under new buildings. Fields, forests, and villages are disappearing under the waters behind huge dams. The population is growing, and people are consuming more than ever before.

One solution to many of these problems is **sustainable development.** This means meeting the needs of people now, without damaging the planet for future generations. Here are some big ideas for a sustainable future.

Interdependence

Our lives are linked to those of other people around the world, by trade, the environment, and **migration**. We should remember this when we make decisions. Decisions taken in one place affect what happens elsewhere. For example, Chinese dams on the upper Mekong river bring the water level too low for people downstream in Thailand to use their boats.

Needs and rights of future generations

We can consider the rights and needs of other people around the world. The actions we take now affect what life will be like in the future. When the first white settlers in the USA ploughed up the thin soils of the Great Plains, they started the process that created the Dust Bowl, which forced their grandchildren to migrate.

Diversity

Cultural, social, economic, and biological diversity is important and valuable. The way of life of the **hunter-gatherers** of Amazonia may seem strange to outsiders, but they have survived for thousands of years without damaging their environment. We should respect that.

Quality of life for everyone

For any development to be sustainable it must benefit people fairly. Development should improve the lives of everyone, not just some at the expense of others. The Chernobyl nuclear power station provided electricity for the people of the Ukraine, but its accident was a disaster for those who lived near by, and forced them to leave their homes and livelihoods.

Residents in Sydney, Australia flee as flames engulf their homes. In 2002, the hot, dry summer, combined with the worst **drought** on record, led to menacing bush fires in the south-eastern states of Australia.

Sustainable change

There is a limit to the way in which the world, particularly the richer countries, can develop. If development is not sustainable and not controlled, poverty will increase and the environment will be damaged. Eventually everyone will lose by this kind of development. Global warming is an example of unsustainable change which may force millions of people to migrate.

Uncertainty and precaution

We are still learning about our environment. Our actions may have unexpected results, as the people of Ireland found in the 19th century when they relied too heavily on potatoes. When the potato crop failed, many people died and many more had to migrate. We should think carefully before we introduce new developments that may affect the environment.

Consider this: sustainability and migration

As we have seen, environmental change can cause migration. A more sustainable world would see less migration. Some of the migrations happening today would be discouraged. For example, the migrants settling in Amazonia and other rainforest areas are destroying these environments. Sustainable development would also reduce poverty, so there would be fewer push factors making poor people want to migrate.

Environmental facts and figures

Environmental migrants

Estimated number of people in poor countries who have had to **migrate** because of environmental change: 12–14 million.

People at risk, today and in the future

These figures show the numbers of people worldwide who are at risk today, and an estimate of how many will be at risk by 2050 or 2080. By 2080 there could be 4 million people in the UK living in homes vulnerable to flooding. Flood damage could cost £20 billion (thousand million) a year.

At risk of malaria:
2001   2400 million people
2080   2690 million people

Suffering from water shortages:
2001   1700 million people
2080   3600 million people

At risk of floods:
2001   520 million people
2050   2000 million people

Carbon dioxide

Carbon dioxide gas in the atmosphere contributes to the greenhouse effect and global warming. These figures show the amount of carbon dioxide released into the atmosphere by each country, in a year. The USA releases 24 per cent of the world's total. Russia releases 17.4 per cent of the world's total.

Country	Emissions of carbon dioxide, in tonnes per year
North America	1,647,753,000
Central Asia	830,859,000
Eastern Europe	775,216,000
South Asia	726,007,000
Western Europe	682,103,000
Oceania	429,040,000
Central and South America and Caribbean	382,344,000
Middle East	363,578,000
Africa	224,371,000

Water quantities

- Over 97 per cent of all the water on Earth is salty.
- Less than 3 per cent of it is fresh.
- 99.5 per cent of the fresh water is locked up in polar ice caps and glaciers.
- 330,000 cubic kilometres (80,000 cubic miles) of water evaporates from the oceans every year.
- 63,000 cubic kilometres (15,000 cubic miles) of water evaporates from the land every year.
- Only 14,000 cubic kilometres (3400 cubic miles) a year of fresh water is available for us to use.

This is because when the water falls back to Earth, as rain or snow, much of it lands in the sea. Also, a lot of the rain that falls on land runs off in rivers before we can use it.

Water usage

Worldwide we use about 3000 cubic kilometres (732 cubic miles) of water every year. This is how we use it:
- **irrigating** land: 73 per cent
- industry: 22 per cent
- domestic use: 5 per cent.

12 per cent of the world's cultivated land is irrigated. That land produces 20 per cent of the world's food.

Everyone needs at least 5 litres (1.1 gallons) of water per day simply to survive. If you include other uses, a person needs at least 30 litres (6.6 gallons) of water per day for drinking, cooking, and washing. Around the world, the amount of water people actually use varies greatly:
- USA: 500 litres per person per day
- India: 25 litres per person per day.

Soil erosion

Every year 24 billion tonnes of topsoil are lost worldwide by **erosion**. That is the same as 11 million hectares (27 million acres) of agricultural land. 25 per cent of all cropland in the USA loses at least two tonnes of soil per hectare (2.5 acres) every year.

Nuclear power

These figures show which countries are the top users of nuclear power. They show the percentage of each country's total electricity output that is produced by nuclear power.

Country	Percentage of electricity produced by nuclear power in 2004
Lithuania	80
France	78
Slovakia	57
Belgium	55
Sweden	50
Ukraine	46
Slovenia	40
South Korea	40
Switzerland	40
Bulgaria	38
Germany	28
Japan	25
UK	24
USA	20

Map of environmental problems and migrations

This map shows the location of environmental problems mentioned in the book. The arrows show the resulting migrations, and possible future migrations.

Arctic Circle

NORTH AMERICA

NORTH ATLANTIC OCEAN

Tropic of Cancer

PACIFIC OCEAN

Equator

SOUTH AMERICA

Tropic of Capricorn

SOUTH ATLANTIC OCEAN

The dust bowl and migration to California

Irish potato famine and migration to Britain and USA

Areas threatened by rising sea level due to global warming

Areas threatened by drought due to global warming

Areas vulnerable to increased storms due to global warming

Tropical rainforests

Possible mass migrations

Antarctic Circle

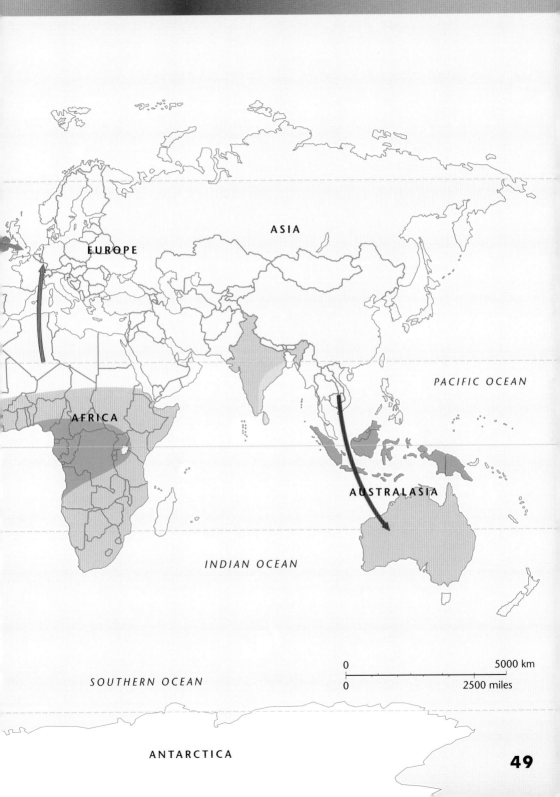

ASIA

EUROPE

PACIFIC OCEAN

AFRICA

AUSTRALASIA

INDIAN OCEAN

0		5000 km
0		2500 miles

SOUTHERN OCEAN

ANTARCTICA

49

Timeline of key events and migrations

79	volcano Vesuvius erupts in southern Italy, killing at least 2000 people
1556	earthquake in Shensi, China kills 830,000 people
1755	earthquake in Lisbon, Portugal kills 60,000 people
1815	volcano Tambora erupts in Indonesia, killing 10,000 people
1845	start of the Irish Potato Famine: 1 million people die, 1.6 million leave Ireland
1869	transcontinental railway is completed across the Great Plains of the USA, bringing a flood of settlers to the west
1883	volcano Krakatoa erupts in Indonesia, killing 36,000 people
1902	volcano Pelée erupts in West Indies, killing 30,000 people
1906	earthquake in San Francisco, USA kills 700 people
1911	volcano Taal erupts in the Philippines, killing 1335 people
1919	volcano Kelut erupts in Indonesia, killing 5110 people
1923	earthquake in Tokyo, Japan kills 156,000 people
1932	start of **drought** in Great Plains of USA: 750,000 people flee the Dust Bowl by the end of the decade
1935	earthquake in Quetta, Pakistan kills 60,000 people
1939	earthquake in Erzincan, Turkey kills 40,000 people
1960	earthquake in Agadir, Morocco kills 14,000 people
1964	earthquake in Anchorage, Alaska kills 125 people
1970	earthquake in Yungay area, Peru kills 65,000 people
1972	earthquake in Managua, Nicaragua kills up to 10,000 people
1976	earthquake in Guatemala City, Guatemala kills 23,000 people
	earthquake in Tangshan, China kills more than 240,000 people
1980	volcano of Mount St Helens erupts in the USA, killing 57 people

1983–1985	famine in Ethiopia: millions of people move to relief camps, but 1 million die of hunger and disease
1985	volcano Nevado del Ruiz erupts in Colombia, killing 23,000 people
	earthquake in Mexico City, Mexico kills 10,000 people
1991	cyclone hits Bangladesh, killing 139,000 people
	volcano Mount Pinatubo erupts in the Philippines: thousands flee the eruption and mudslide
1998	Hurricane Mitch hits Central America and southern Mexico, killing 11,000 people; it makes 1.3 million people homeless in Honduras
	floods hit Bangladesh, affecting 30 million people
2001	earthquake in Gujarat, India kills 20,000 people
	40,000 people are **evacuated** because of fears of flood from the crater lake in Mount Pinatubo, Philippines
2002	floods in Europe kill 100 people, and affect 450,000
	Lee Raymond, Chairman of the Exxon Mobil oil company, says: "We in Exxon Mobil do not believe that the science required to establish this linkage between **fossil fuels** and warming has been demonstrated."
2003	earthquake in Bam, Iran kills 30,000 people
2004	Ron Oxburgh, Chairman of the Shell oil company, says: "No one can be comfortable at the prospect of continuing to pump out the amounts of carbon dioxide that we are at present. People are going to go on allowing this atmospheric carbon dioxide to build up, with consequences that we really can't predict, but are probably not good."
	floods in Bangladesh leave nearly 800 people dead, damage 4 million homes and destroy over a million hectares (2.5 million acres) of crops.
	floods caused by Hurricane Jeanne kill 2000 people in Haiti
	Indian Ocean tsunmai kills more than 200,000 people. The tsunami also destroys the homes and livelihoods of many millions.

Glossary

basalt hard rock formed from cooled lava

crust solid surface of the Earth, a layer of rock about 20 miles thick

decontaminate remove contamination, usually radioactive materials of poisonous chemicals, from clothes, buildings, land, or objects

delta a big river can form a delta when it reaches the sea. It splits up into many channels, with flat, flood-prone land between them. The Nile, Ganges, and Mississippi rivers have deltas.

development countries become richer by economic development. They build factories, roads, dams, and power stations, produce more goods, and use more raw materials. Development should also mean that people are better-off, better educated, and in better health.

drainage ditches man-made channels to drain water away from a swampy or flood-prone area

drought long period of time, lasting many months or even years, where there is little or no rainfall

dyke raised artificial bank, often built alongside a river to prevent floods

economy a country's economy is created by the work people do, the money they spend, and the goods and services they produce

embankment man-made wall of earth alongside a river, to prevent the river overflowing and flooding the surrounding land

emigration migration out of a country

environment everything around us, both natural and man-made: soil, air, water, plants and animals, buildings, farms, and cities

erosion natural process that wears away rock or soil, by water, wind, sand, or rain

evacuation moving people away from their homes for a time because of fears for their safety

fertility goodness in soil that produces good crops

fossil fuels coal, oil, and natural gas, which developed from the fossils of prehistoric plants and animals

fungal disease disease caused by a microscopic fungus

geology study of Earth's features, such as rocks, soils, mountains, rivers, and oceans

groundwater underground water which has soaked down through the soil, flows slowly through layers of rock, and emerges at springs

hunter-gatherers people who hunt animals, catch fish, and gather plant foods. They move around with the seasons to find food.

Ice Ages periods in Earth's history when ice sheets covered much of the surface

immigration migration into a country

indigenous people original inhabitants of an area, for instance the Native Americans of Amazonia

industrial an industrial economy is one in which most things are made in factories, and most people work in industry, rather than in agriculture. Industrialization is the change in a country's economy from mainly agricultural to mainly industrial activity.

intensive agriculture farming which gets as big a crop as possible by use of irrigation, fertilizers, and chemical sprays to kill weeds and pests

irrigation supplying water for agriculture, either to grow crops where none were possible or to grow more crops by creating a more reliable supply of water

mass extinctions When a plant or animal species dies out, it becomes extinct. At various stages in the Earth's history, many species have become extinct at around the same time. This is known as mass extinction.

migration movement of people, especially in large numbers, from one country to another, or from one part of a country to another

monsoon a wind that brings heavy rainfall over parts of Asia

protein foods our bodies need to build and repair themselves, such as meat, fish, cheese, and beans

radioactive radioactive elements emit energy in the form of heat, X-rays, or other radiation. These emissions can often be very dangerous to humans.

reservation area set aside for a group of people to live in, especially for Native Americans in the USA

sediment solid material, such as sand and mud, carried by a river to the sea

silt sediment dropped by a river, especially at the delta where the river meets the sea

sustainable able to last. Sustainable development means meeting the needs of people now, without damaging the planet for future generations.

thyroid gland which controls growth. The thyroid is very vulnerable to damage from radiation.

tropics area of the world between the Tropic of Cancer and the Tropic of Capricorn. The climate in the tropics is hot all the year round. Some parts of the tropics are very dry, others have very high rainfall.

tsunami huge, destructive wave crossing the ocean, caused by an earthquake on the sea bed or by the explosion of an island volcano

ultraviolet rays radiation whose wavelength is less than that of visible light.

Further resources

Websites
International Organization for Migration
www.iom.int

Centre for Migration Studies, New York
www.cmsny.org

National Centre for Migration Studies, University of Aberdeen, Scotland
www.ini.smo.uhi.ac.uk/contact.htm

An authoritative website on climate change
www.ipcc.ch

A sceptical view on climate change
www.scienceforum.net

Environmental organizations
Friends of the Earth: www.foe.co.uk
Greenpeace: www.greenpeace.org.uk
WWF-UK: www.wwf.org.uk

Worldaware works in the UK to raise awareness of international
development issues
www.worldaware.org.uk

Charities working to reduce poverty
Oxfam: www.oxfam.org.uk
Christian Aid: www.christian-aid.org.uk
Save the Children: www.savethechildren.org.uk

Australian Organizations
Australian Conservation Foundation: www.acfonline.org.au

Department of Immigration, Multicultural and Indigenous affairs:
www.immi.gov.au

World Wildlife Fund: www.wwf.org.au

Save the Children: www.savethechildren.org.au

Friends of the Earth: www.foe.org.au

Greenpeace: www.greenpeace.org.au

Further reading

Brown, Paul, *Just The Facts: Global Pollution*, (Heinemann Library, 2002)

Dalal, Anita, *Nations of the World: Brazil*, (Raintree, 2004)

Dalton, Dave, *People on the Move: Economic Migrants*, (Heinemann Library, 2006)

Dalton, Dave, *People on the Move: Nomads and Travellers*, (Heinemann Library, 2006)

Dalton, Dave, *People on the Move: Refugees and Asylum Seekers*, (Heinemann Library, 2006)

Jackson, Tom, *Biomes Atlases: Tropical Forests*, (Raintree, 2003)

Litvinoff, Miles, *Atlas of Earthcare: A Guide to Looking After Our Planet*, (Gaia Books, 1996)

Middleton, Nick, *The Global Casino: An Introduction to Environmental Issues*, (Arnold, 2003)

Pollock, David C. and Van Reken, Ruth E., *Third Culture Kids: The Experience of Growing Up Among Worlds*, (Intercultural Press, 2001)

Scoones, Simon, *21st Century Debates: Climate Change*, (Hodder Wayland, 2004)

Stalker, Peter, *The No-Nonsense Guide to International Migration*, (Verso Books, 2001)

Steinbeck, John, *The Grapes of Wrath*, (Penguin Books, 2001)
This 1939 novel is about migrants from The Dust Bowl in the USA, and what happened to them in California.

Index